F O R R E S T   W I L S O N 1918-

What It Feels Like To Be A Building

Landmark Reprint Series

The Preservation Press

National Trust
for Historic Preservation

The Preservation Press
National Trust for Historic Preservation
1785 Massachusetts Avenue, N.W.
Washington, D.C. 20036

Library of Congress Cataloging in Publication Data

Wilson, Forrest, 1918–
    What it feels like to be a building.

    (Landmark reprint series)
    Summary: Explains how different parts of a building, such as columns, walls, beams, buttresses, rods and cables, function to support great weight and stress.
    1. Structural engineering — Juvenile literature.   2. Buildings — Juvenile literature.
[1. Buildings   2. Structural engineering]
I. Title.   II. Series
TA634.W55   1988   690'.21   88-22382
ISBN 0-89133-142-5
ISBN 0-89133-147-6 (pbk.)

Edited by Diane Maddex, director, and Janet Walker, managing editor, The Preservation Press

Designed by Robert Wiser and Marc Alain Meadows, Meadows & Wiser, Washington, D.C.

Composed in ITC Century by General Typographers, Inc., Washington, D.C.
Printed on 80-pound Mohawk Superfine by the John D. Lucas Printing Company, Baltimore, Md.

For my wife and my children, Jonathan, Robert and Paul.
And for my students, who for so many years
have so kindly and graciously allowed me to think
that I was teaching them while they were teaching me.

Building Body Language

Everyone can understand buildings. You feel gravity,
wind, sun and rain. Buildings feel the same stresses
and strains that people do. For this reason
you can put yourself in a building's place.
When you feel what it feels like to be a building,
you can talk to buildings and they will talk to you
in building body language.

Buildings stand up because gravity pulls them down

toward the center of the earth.

Gravity feels like glue.

If it did not, stones would fly.

It feels like SQUASH to be a column,
because columns
are squashed between a building and the ground.

Even though a column might be disguised in squiggles,
it still feels squashed.

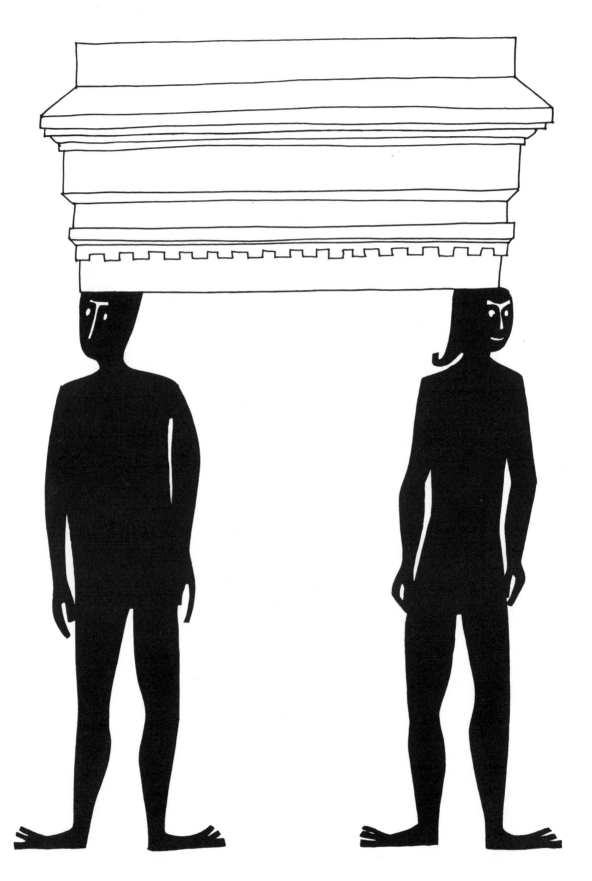

Columns must stand straight up as they push straight down
to carry the weight of a building to the ground.

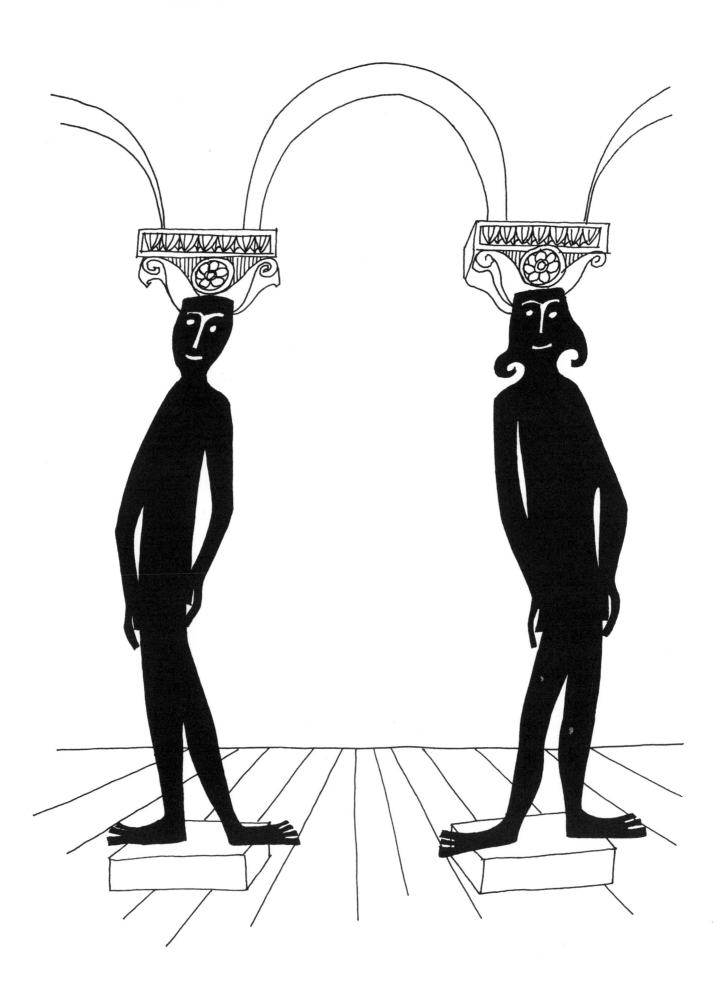

Long thin columns tend to bend,

short to shatter.

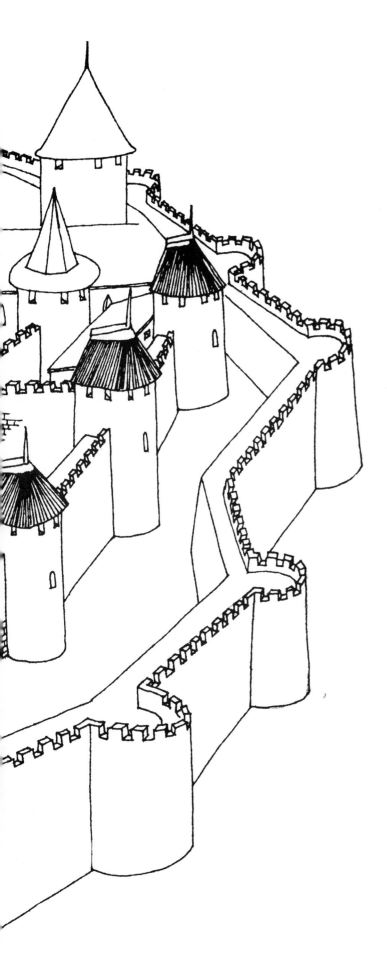

Walls do the same thing that columns do, only more.

It feels like multiple SQUASH to be a wall,
because being wider and longer than a column,
a wall carries more of a building's weight to the ground.

The ground must push up as hard as columns and walls push down,

although sometimes columns and walls push harder.

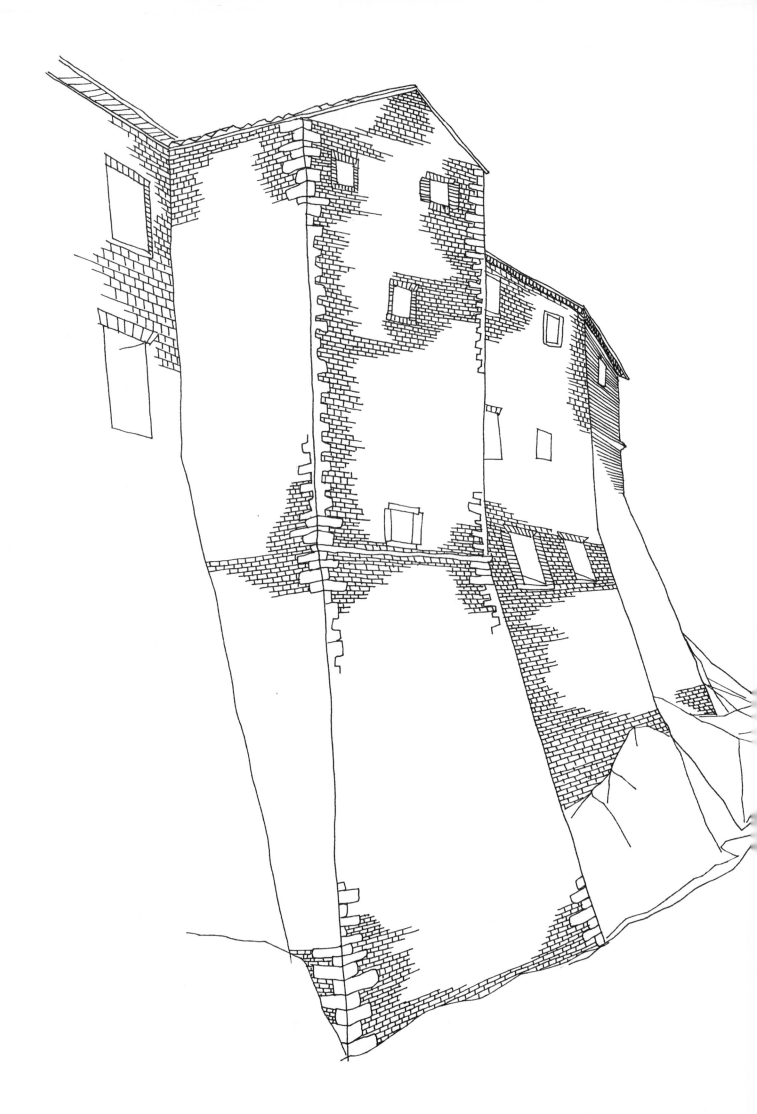

Buildings must get stronger near the bottom,
because the closer they get to the ground,
the more weight they carry over their heads.

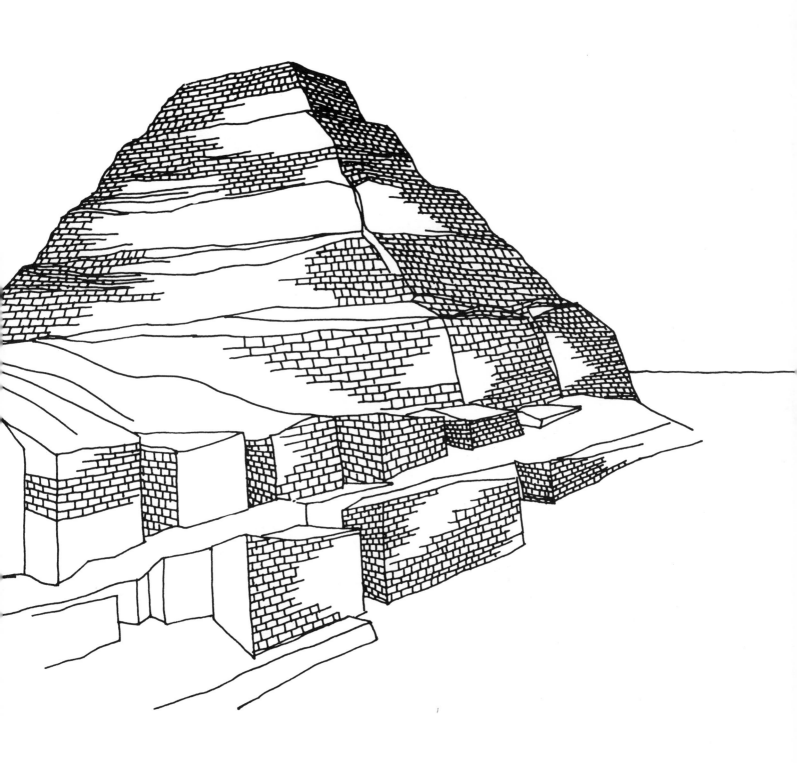

This is why pyramids are wider at the bottom than they are at the top.

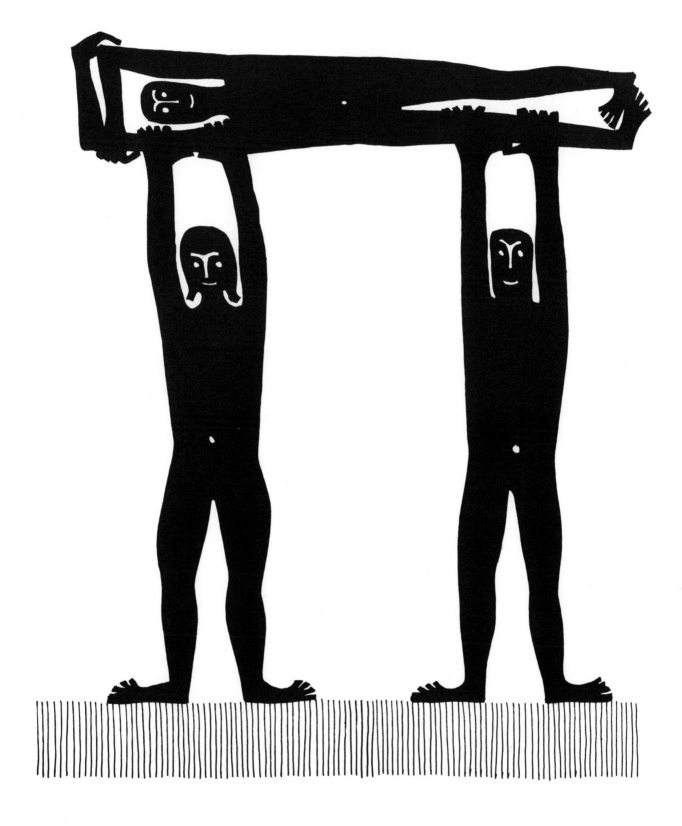

It feels like *BEND* to be a beam, because

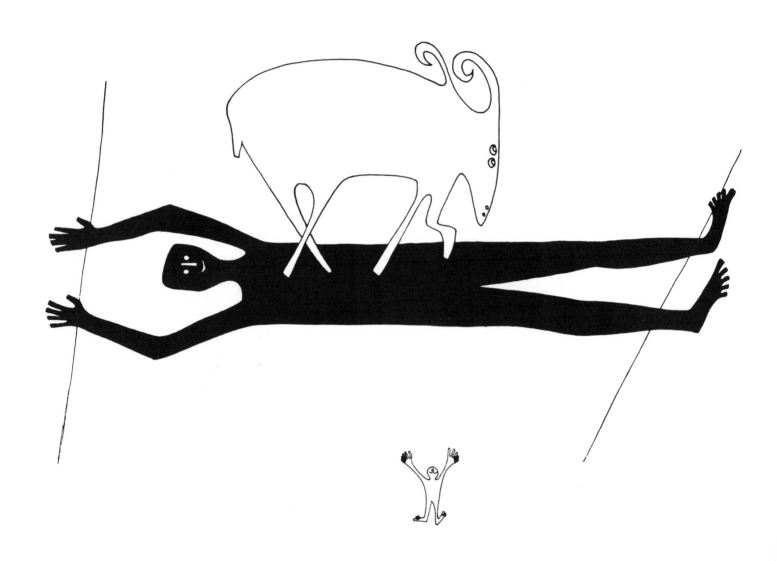

the beam does not, like the column and the wall,

carry weight straight down.

It carries the weight across to its supports.

This makes the top of the beam feel like getting shorter
by pushing together and its bottom feel like
getting longer by pulling apart.

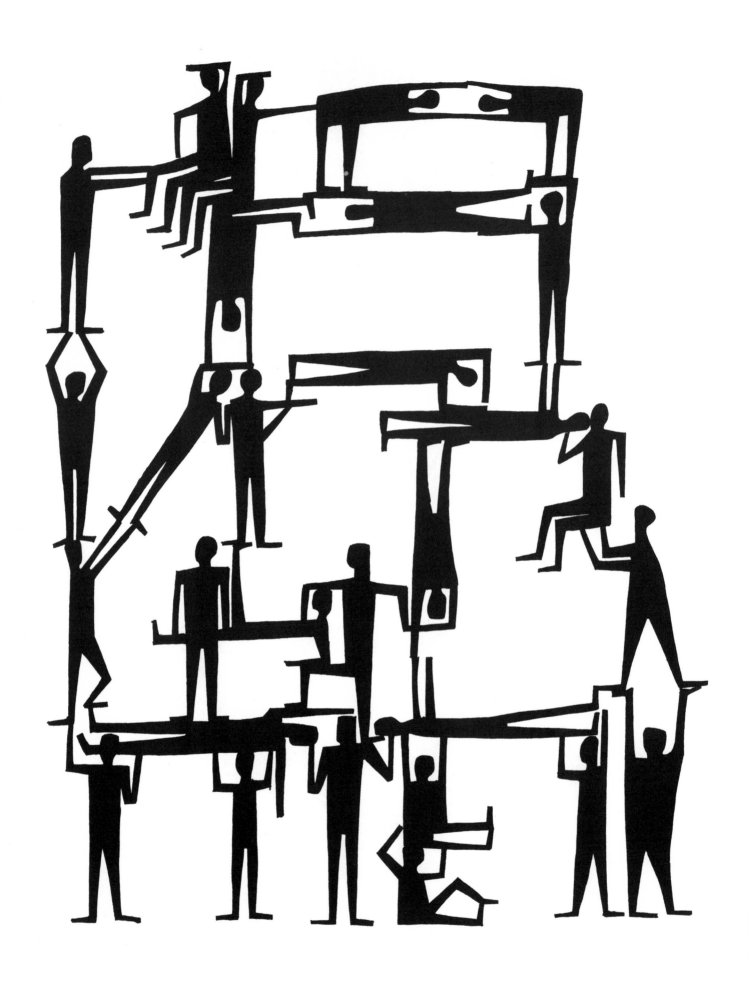

But beams cannot bend too much because they would split in the middle.

This is why roofs supported by beams are flat.

Sometimes beams are inclined to butt,

but they push and pull to stay straight even when placed at an angle.

This is what it feels like to be a house with beams on an angle,

resting on walls that stand straight up as they push straight down.

A Greek temple has the same feeling as a house,
only much more serious. It has very important columns standing up
while pushing straight down, with short, strong, straight beams
between the columns and impressive butting beams over all of this.

If you felt like a Greek temple, you would feel very important,
but you would still feel squashed, bent and inclined to butt.

It feels like DROOP to be a corbel, because corbels are not very ambitious. They are content to carry just a little bit of the load at a time.

The word "corbel" comes from the Latin word "corvus"
for raven or crow, which is quite sensible
because crows are corbelled at both ends.

A corbel is dogged.

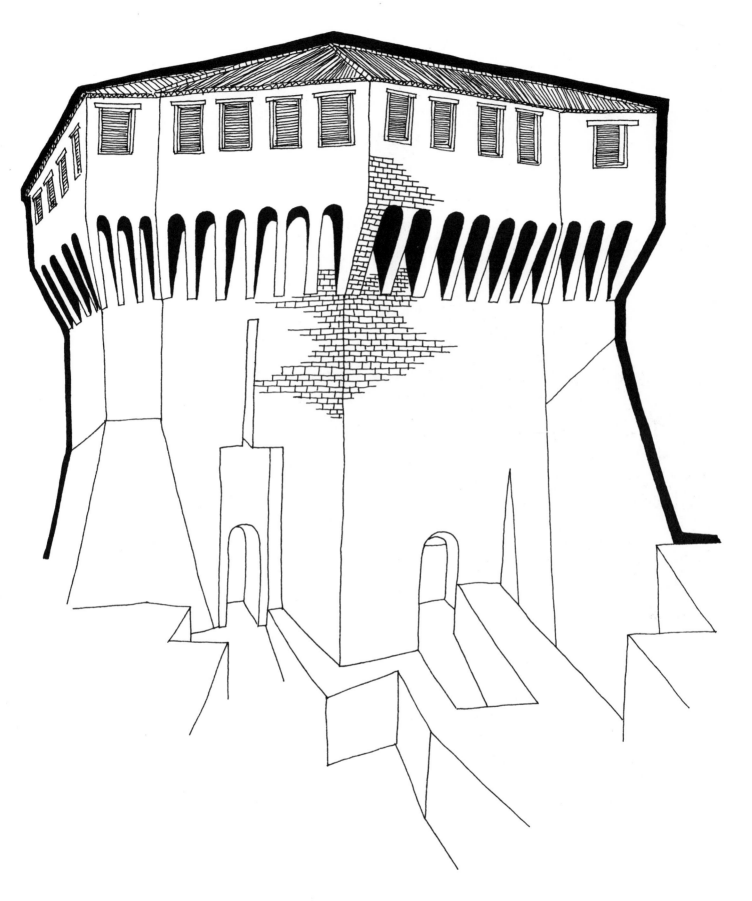

Corbels stubbornly push out, bit by bit,

in little upside-down steps,

as they carry the load back to a building's walls.

It feels like SQUEEZE to be an arch, because an arch
is all squeeze-push with no pull at all.

Rounded forms in buildings show that squeezing arches are at work.

Arches squeeze around these windows in a tower,

which stands straight up while being pulled straight down.

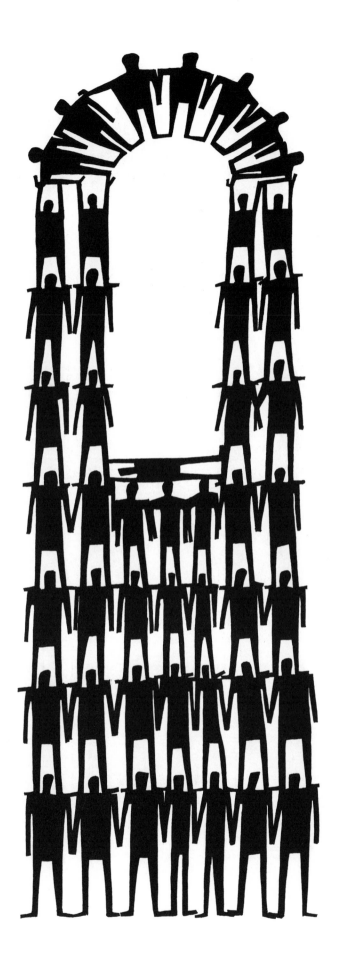

This is how an arched window in a tower feels.

Domes, like a circle of arches,

feel like multiple **SQUEEZE** because they push in all directions.

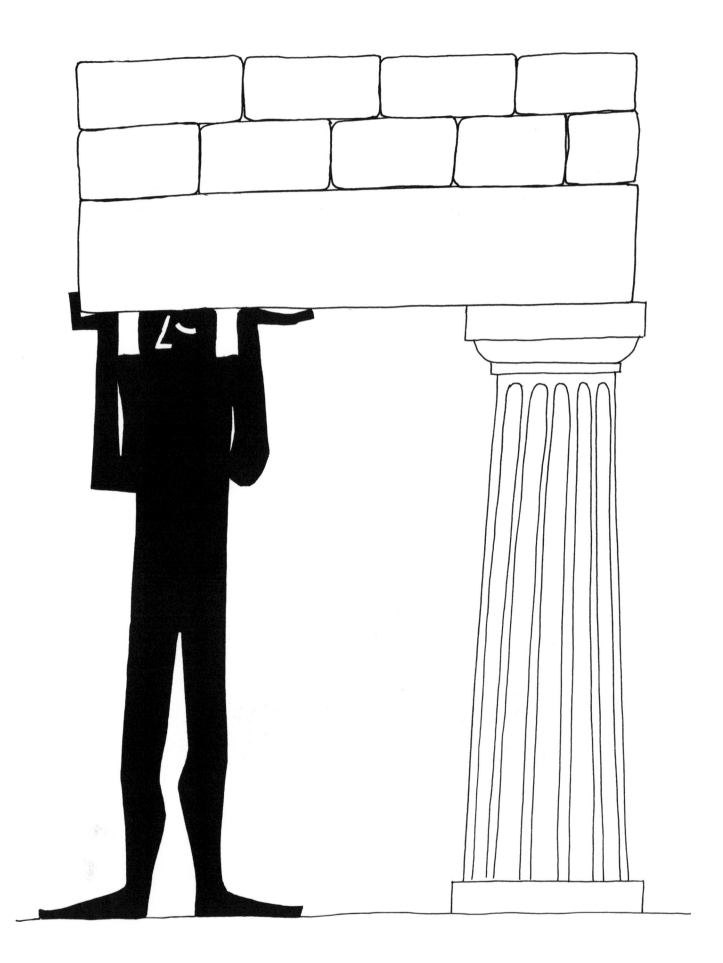

Columns nap.

Walls doze.

Corbels drowse.

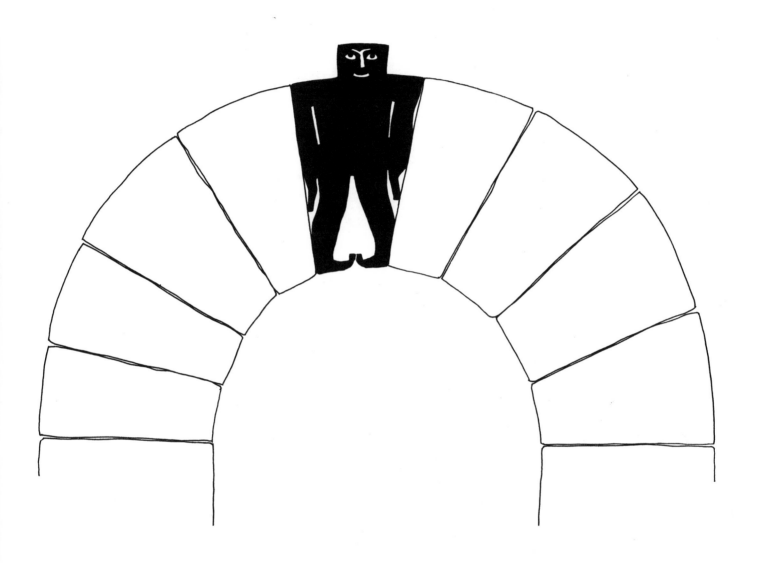

But the arch never sleeps.

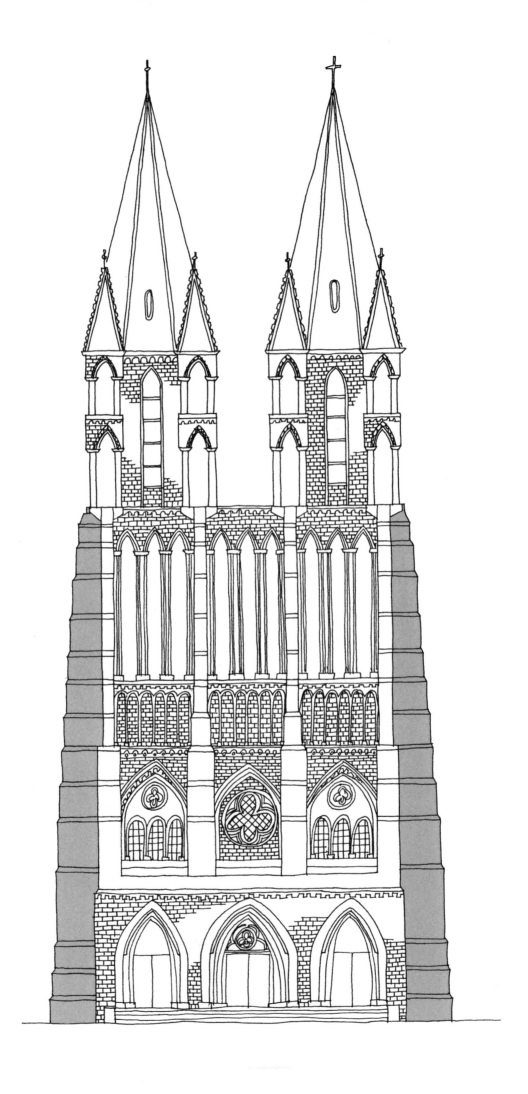

It feels like *BRACE* to be a buttress,

because a buttress supports a building's walls.

A buttress pushes in against a wall at exactly the place

where the wall feels most like pushing out.

This would happen

if buttresses did not push in.

This is a tower of walls and buttresses and butting beams.

Four butting beams
make a pointed tower top,

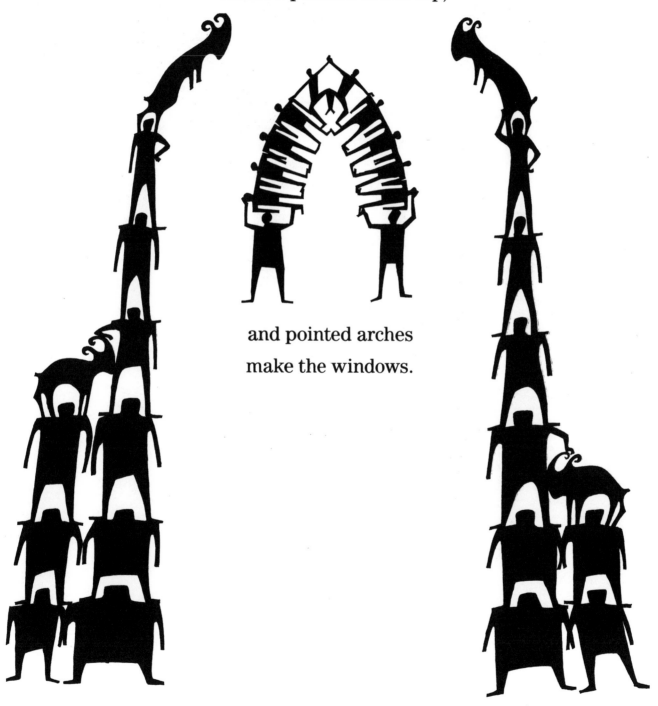

and pointed arches
make the windows.

Buttresses hold up the tower walls.

A flying buttress is the arch's cousin.

It is like half an arch that flies from its support
to brace a wall in the air.

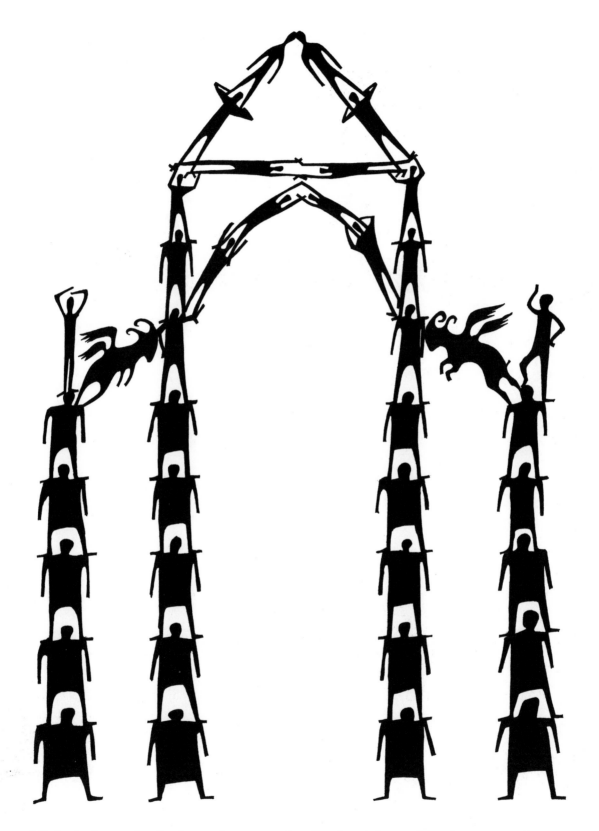

This is how it feels to be a cathedral with walls that stand up
while they push straight down, topped by butting beams that push out
and flying buttresses that take to the air to push them back again.

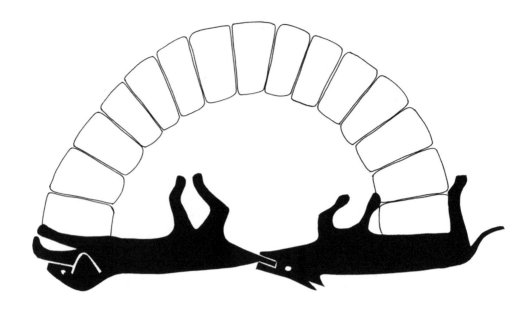

It feels like *TUG* to be a rod,
because rods can use their pull to do what buttresses do
with their push. They pull in exactly the places

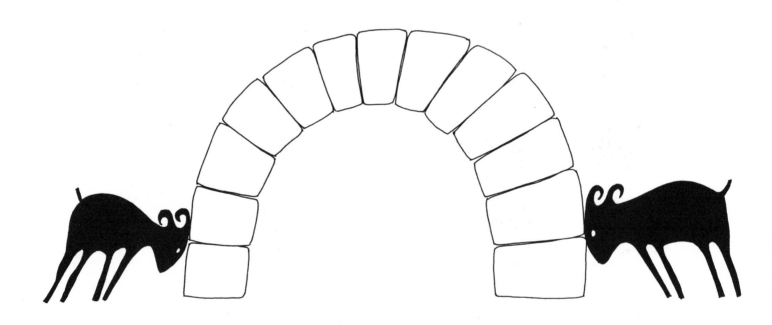

where buttresses would push.

Cables are relaxed when things are slack,

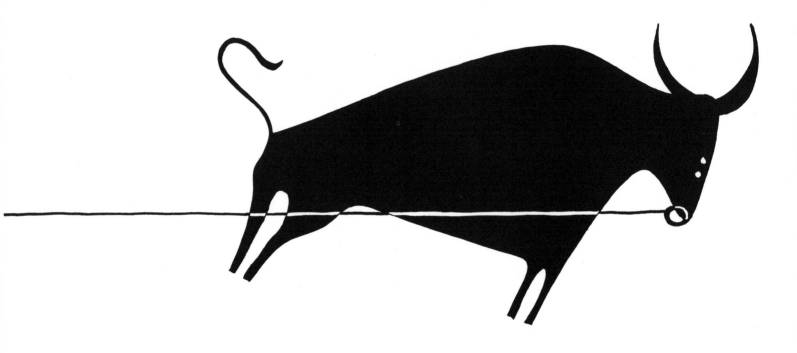

but when you see the pull of tension,

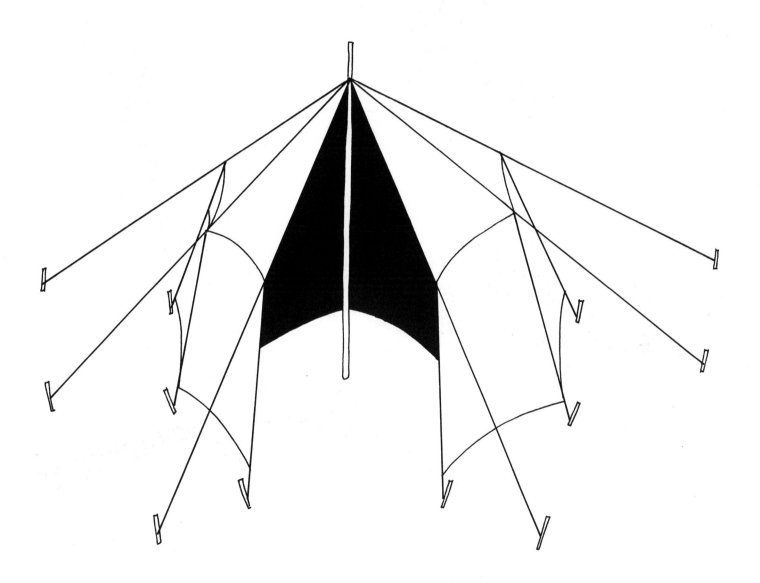

you know that cables are working.

So, *PUSH*

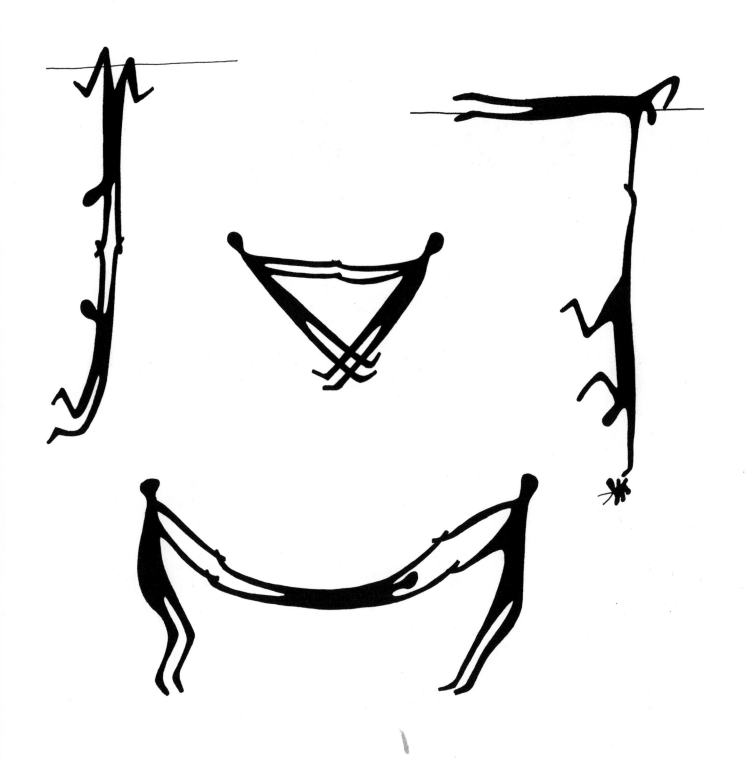

or PULL

or

SQUASH

SQUEEZE

DROOP

TUG

BEND

or

BRACE,

that's what it feels like to be a building!

Forrest Wilson

Forrest Wilson earned his carpenter's union card while working his way through the California School of Fine Arts, where he studied architectural sculpture. He has been a ship's carpenter, construction superintendent, professor of architectural design and construction, editor of *Progressive Architecture*, director of the School of Architecture, Design and Planning at Ohio University, associate dean of the School of Engineering and Architecture and chairman of the Department of Architecture at The Catholic University of America. He has written numerous articles and 16 books on architecture, design and building for children and adults, including *Architecture: A Book of Projects for Young Adults* and *City Planning: The Game of Human Settlements*.

Wilson is professor emeritus of The Catholic University, Washington, D.C., visiting professor at The Catholic University and the University of Maryland, and senior editor for technology for *Architecture*, the journal of the American Institute of Architects.

Related Books from The Preservation Press

Archabet: An Architectural Alphabet
Photographs by Balthazar Korab

Archabet juxtaposes dramatic photographs of all 26 letters — hidden among facades and doorways — with quotations by architectural observers from Goethe to Wright. The letters reveal themselves in styles ranging from Victorian gingerbread to angular lines of steel. "Perhaps those who will most appreciate *Archabet* are the wise and the young." — *Architecture.* Included in the Art Directors Club of New York *Design 88* calendar. 64 pages, 52 illus. 8″ x 8″ $14.95 hb age 10 and up

Architects Make Zigzags:
Looking at Architecture from A to Z
Drawings by Roxie Munro

"Zigzags are strings of M's, W's or Z's that zig and zag together like a chorus line around a building," explains this fanciful introduction to the ABCs of architecture. *New Yorker* cover artist Roxie Munro's whimsical line drawings of real buildings will delight readers of all ages. Architectural terms depicted in the drawings — such as gable, keystone and quoin — are defined in easy-to-understand language. "Quite literally, the book sets out to draw children into the preservation field." — *Christian Science Monitor.* An *American Bookseller* "Pick of the List." 64 pages, 48 illus., biblio. 8″ x 8½″ $8.95 pb age 8 and up

I Know That Building!
Discovering Architecture with Activities and Games
Jane D'Alelio

This unique and colorful activity book brings the world of architecture right into a child's own home. *I Know That Building!* presents 30 projects — puzzles, quizzes, games, models to make and pages to color — ranging from "Go Build" (a game about architects) to a rubbing of an elaborate manhole cover (embossed on the book's back cover). In between are a covered bridge to cut and assemble, skyscrapers to construct, a diorama of a one-room schoolhouse to put together and a mosaic to restore. On Main Street, a new building waits to be designed. A Queen Anne house is ready to be dressed with roofs and a porch. A ghost town slowly reveals the secrets of its past. Other projects, based on actual historic places, introduce children to architectural styles, terminology, periods and materials.

A special gift for parents, grandparents, relatives and friends to give to children, this activity book — filled with pages meant to be well used — will develop an interest in buildings to last a lifetime. 88 pages, 200 color and b/w illus. 9″ x 12″ $12.95 pb age 8 and up

What Style Is It?
A Guide to American Architecture
John Poppeliers, S. Allen Chambers, Jr., and Nancy B. Schwartz
Historic American Buildings Survey

What Style Is It? will help "anyone interested in identifying and enjoying the architectural assets of a building" *(New York Times).* Already a classic, this concise book has introduced tens of thousands of Americans to the architectural styles that surround them, from Gothic Revival and Richardsonian Romanesque to Prairie School and Art Deco. 112 pages, 150 illus., gloss., biblio. 4¼″ x 10″ $7.95 pb

To order, send the total of the book prices (less 10 percent discount for National Trust members), plus $3 postage and handling, to: Mail Order, National Trust for Historic Preservation, 1600 H Street, N.W., Washington, D.C. 20006. Residents of California, Colorado, Washington, D.C., Illinois, Iowa, Louisiana, Maryland, Massachusetts, New York, Pennsylvania, South Carolina, Texas and Virginia please add applicable sales tax. Please make checks payable to the National Trust or provide your credit card number, expiration date, signature and telephone number.